SCOTNOTES
Number 3

George Douglas Brown's
The House with the Green Shutters

Iain Crichton Smith

Association for Scottish Literary Studies 1988

Published by
Association for Scottish Literary Studies
c/o Department of Scottish History
9 University Gardens
University of Glasgow
Glasgow G12 8QH

www.asls.org.uk

First published 1988
Reprinted 2000, 2002, 2006

© The Estate of Iain Crichton Smith

A CIP catalogue for this title is available from the British Library

ISBN: 0 948877 03 0
ISBN-13: 978 0 948877 03 2

The Association for Scottish Literary Studies
is in receipt of subsidy from the Scottish Arts Council

Printed by Ritchie (UK) Ltd, Kilmarnock

CONTENTS

Editors' Foreword	v
Acknowledgements	vii
Note on References	viii
SUMMARY	1
THE LIFE OF GEORGE DOUGLAS BROWN	6
CHARACTERISATION	9
STRUCTURE	16
LANGUAGE	21
AN ESTIMATE OF THE NOVEL	26
NOTES	33
FOR FURTHER STUDY	34
BIBLIOGRAPHY	35
GLOSSARY	36

EDITORS' FOREWORD

The *Scotnotes* booklets are a series of study guides to major Scottish writers and literary texts that are likely to be elements within literature courses. They are aimed at senior pupils in secondary schools and students in further education colleges and colleges of education. Each booklet in the series is written by a person who is not only an authority on the particular writer or text but also experienced in teaching at the relevant levels in schools or colleges. Furthermore, the editorial board, composed of members of the Schools and Further Education Committee of the Association for Scottish Literary Studies, considers the suitability of each booklet for the students in question.

For many years there has been a shortage of readily accessible critical notes for the general student of Scottish literature. *Scotnotes* has grown as a series to meet this need, and provides students with valuable aids to the understanding and appreciation of the key writers and major texts within the Scottish literary tradition.

Lorna Borrowman Smith
Ronald Renton

ACKNOWLEDGEMENTS

I should like to express my indebtedness to *Nineteenth-Century Scottish Fiction, a Critical Anthology*, edited by Ian Campbell and in particular to Dr Campbell's essay in that volume, 'George Douglas Brown. A Study in Objectivity'.

NOTE ON REFERENCES

Throughout this study guide, the page references given for quotations from *The House with the Green Shutters* are to the Penguin Classics edition (1985), edited by Dorothy Porter. Other references are to be found on page 34.

SUMMARY

(a) Chapters 1-8

The book begins with a description of a morning in Barbie which appears calm and peaceful though this, as we shall see later, is a false assumption. The carts which belong to Gourlay are about to set out. Gourlay himself is shown at the height of his powers, commanding, prosperous, dominating the town.

We are told that he has the carrying trade completely in his hands, having leased the quarry from Templandmuir, the local laird. Yet at the same time, because of his proud nature, he has made enemies, and we are introduced to a number of them who are called the 'bodies' in the novel and are the kind of people who are continually sarcastic and cutting. Gourlay, however, can outface them with his House with the Green Shutters which is the best house in the town, situated prominently at the top of the brae. It is the pride of Gourlay's life.

Yet all is not satisfactory as might appear. Gourlay's wife is slatternly and untidy and spends a lot of her time reading novels. His daughter, Janet, is poor in health and his son, John, is idle, though doted on by his mother. There follows an incident where the son causes a quarrel with Gilmour whom Gourlay dismisses on the spot, partly at the instigation of his wife.

The author then gives us a more detailed insight into the minds of the 'bodies' who are shown as spiteful and inveterately hostile to Gourlay. They welcome Gilmour as he meets them after his dismissal but, though outwardly pleasant to him, they gossip about him maliciously as soon as his back is turned. One of their reasons for hating Gourlay is that there is no 'give-and-take' in him and that he treats them like dirt. We also discover that Gourlay married his wife for her money. The 'bodies' ask Gourlay if he will allow water for the benefit of the town to pass through his garden but Gourlay contemptuously refuses. He has no interest in the community at all. Johnny Coe tells a story of Gourlay's courage, how one night of lightning and storm he had brought the doctor home to his wife who was then in childbirth with young John. They are awed by this story but soon forget it in their conviction that young John is a dunce anyway.

Young John is then seen going to school. He hates school

and is always being beaten by the master. He is an imaginative boy but at the same time not very clever. He boasts to the other boys about the new kitchen range, but naturally they don't like this and they bully him. He is about to have a fight with Swipey, son of the local rag-and-bone merchant, when he suddenly turns and runs. When he arrives home his mother protects him and doesn't tell his father that he is playing truant. He hides in the garret and reads a book though he doesn't particularly like reading. Janet threatens to tell his father but he threatens her in turn. This shows his own bullying nature and his cowardice, since he only threatens people weaker than himself. When he comes down, his father is showing the range to a friend of his, a prosperous farmer. There is an incident with a poker which will be of importance later in the book.

(b) Chapters 9-13

While he is watching his carts, Gourlay sees a stranger coming up the street. The stranger greets him politely, but Gourlay in his usual surly way insults him, the more so when he hears that he is John Wilson, son of the town mole-catcher. Gourlay's contemptuous treatment of this man makes him a permanent enemy and, though Gourlay does not know it, this signals the beginning of the end of his domination of Barbie.

Wilson sets up business in the town. He has made some money in Aberdeen and, hearing about the possible opening of mines in Barbie, has decided that there are possibilities in the area. He has a hard-working wife and son who help him in his business and who contrast strongly with Gourlay's wife and son. Wilson is not content with the Emporium that he opens; he sees other opportunities for expansion. He becomes a collector of eggs, butter and cheese for merchants; he initiates a hire-purchase system; he carries coal for customers. This entry into the carrying trade brings him into direct confrontation with Gourlay. From here on Gourlay and Wilson become bitter rivals and are seen to be so by the 'bodies', who regard Wilson as an instrument by which they can get their own back on Gourlay.

Troubles now begin to assail Gourlay. Templandmuir, who owns the quarry, has now married and his wife urges him to take the lease away from Gourlay. When he comes to visit Gourlay to discuss the renewal of the lease he will not take a drink as usual and says that he is going to a meeting which has been called about the railway and in which Wilson takes a leading part. Gourlay, though recognising the advantages the railway will bring, opposes it because of Wilson's prominence in the enterprise. Templandmuir doesn't and dissociates himself from Gourlay, picks a quarrel and ends the lease of the quarry. Gourlay is so angry he hits his wife and sets off the disease — cancer of the breast — that will ruin her health.

The pressure is now kept on Gourlay by his enemies in the town among whom a man named Gibson, whom Gourlay has antagonised in the past, is pre-eminent. Gibson and Wilson concoct a plot to destroy Gourlay. It is an intricate, clever plan which deceives Gourlay. When he finds out the full implications of it he physically attacks Gibson and throws him through a window, thus involving himself in a lawsuit which consumes a large part of his money.

(c) Chapters 14-21

The novel now focusses on young Gourlay who is sent by his father to the High School of Skeighan, but he only learns to smoke and drink and remains as idle as ever. One particular incident when he is playing truant in the waiting-room of the railway station shows his cowardice. There is a tremendous thunder storm. Young Gourlay cowers and screams. This scene contrasts strongly with the one where Gourlay senior outfaces the storm to bring the doctor to his wife. It also reveals the sensitivity of young Gourlay's imagination. His father finds him and takes him back to school where he demands that the headmaster gives him a thrashing.

In spite of his physical bravery, however, Gourlay senior is confused by the machinations of modern business. He is outwitted at every turn by Wilson and is continually losing money. His pony dies and he has to take the public gig into Skeighan. Some of the 'bodies' on the gig enrage Gourlay by their sly comments about slatternly wives, stupid sons and successful businessmen like Wilson. The result of all this is to impel Gourlay to the most disastrous decision he has yet taken, the sending of his son to University, even though his old teacher says of young Gourlay: 'They're making a great mistake ... Yon boy's the last youngster on earth who should go to College.' (p. 142).

Young Gourlay is indeed unfitted for University. He has hardly seen anything of the world and going to Edinburgh frightens him, since he so much prefers the familiar to the unfamiliar. Furthermore, he has no academic ability to allow him to cope with the demands of the University. He is lonely, low-spirited and bored. He is 'rescued' from his isolation by Jock Allan who had once been in love with Gourlay's mother and is now an actuary in Edinburgh. Allan is the centre of a group of students and other young men who talk in an affected manner, thinking that they are very clever. Young Gourlay can only hold his own in their company by the false confidence given to him by drink.

There is a prize given annually by the University called the Raeburn Prize which has a great deal of prestige. Using his undoubted power of imagination, Gourlay wins the prize which makes him think that he doesn't need to work to get a degree. His father is delighted especially when young Wilson, though much cleverer, fails to win anything.

After winning the Raeburn, young Gourlay drinks even more heavily but is flattered by the attention he receives not only from the 'bodies' who encourage him to drink, but also from the minister who has a nostalgic love of his own days at the University. The latter also encourages him by his praise to think that he is an exceptional man. The six month vacation, usual in those days, confirms young Gourlay in his drinking habits. He plays the part of the man of the world who is also a genius.

(d) Chapters 21-25

While young Gourlay is spending his money on drink and cigars, his father's business is failing. He even has to sack Peter Riney, his last and oldest servant. The scene in which he does this is very touching. Peter muses that he may end in the poorhouse and with uncharacteristic generosity Gourlay gives him some money that he can ill afford. The departure of Riney signals the lowest point in Gourlay's fortunes. Now all he has left is the possible success of his only son.

But this is not to be. During an uproarious lecture, the lecturer, being unable to exercise any control, singles young Gourlay out for punishment. Asked to apologise, he refuses, feeling it is unfair that he should have been picked on when others were equally guilty. Because of his stubbornness and refusal to compromise, he is sent home in disgrace. Now he has to face his father for whose financial ruin the 'bodies' are eagerly awaiting, since he is now reduced to borrowing money on the House with the Green Shutters, his pride and joy. Even Coe refuses to lend him money. His anger at Barbie, at his son, is uncontrollable.

Inevitably, the meeting between Gourlay and his son is a stormy one. Young Gourlay is terrified by the depth of his father's anger and his father in turn is disgusted by his son's cowardice. In a wild humour, he sets out glasses for drink and sarcastically serves his son. After he has forced him to drink a large amount of whisky, he taunts him in an almost maniacal manner. His mother tells him to run out of the house, which he does, but only to drink more in the local pub. With the false courage of drink, he returns to the house. In the ensuing argument, young Gourlay kills his father with the poker.

(e) Chapters 26-27

In his drunken delirium and guilt, young Gourlay begins to have hallucinations. A letter arrives saying that the mortgage on the house is not being paid. In spite of being pursued by the 'eyes' of his father, young Gourlay goes to Glasgow to see the lawyers. When he comes back, drunk, he tells his mother that indeed the house is in danger of being taken away from them. Young Gourlay buys a lethal mixture of whisky and poison and kills himself. His mother and Janet also commit suicide with the remains of the poison. The bodies are discovered by the postman who has entered the house to get payment for an understamped letter.

The book, therefore, ends in a multiple tragedy. The last sentence refers to the House with the Green Shutters sitting there 'dark and terrible' while the indifferent dawn rises.

THE LIFE OF GEORGE DOUGLAS BROWN

We want to know about an author's life for one important reason, that by learning of it we might attain a greater insight into his work.

George Douglas Brown was born in Ochiltree, Ayrshire, in 1869, the illegitimate son of Sarah Gemmell and George Douglas Brown, a farmer who lived quite near Ochiltree. His mother walked out of the farm to have her baby on her own after some of the father's relatives objected to his being involved with an 'Irish servant'.

The future author attended the village school at Ochiltree but, when his mother became dairymaid to a Coylton farmer, he transferred to Coylton School. Although he liked school and was successful as a pupil, George Douglas Brown felt he had to leave school at twelve to earn money and help his mother. He found work 'craw picking' at a pithead, that is, separating stones and dirt from coal. But since he continued to read and study, it was easy for him to return to school when he and his mother moved, first of all to Ochiltree and then to Cronberry. Later, he attended Ayr Academy where he impressed the Rector by his knowledge of literature.

At Glasgow University he won a medal for Greek, graduated M.A. in 1890 with First Class Honours in Classics and was awarded the Eglinton Classical Fellowship. At the end of his post-graduate year at Glasgow University, he was awarded the Snell Exhibition entitling him to £130 for three years at Oxford where he spent more time reading English literature than studying the Classics. During the next two years, his mother became seriously ill and he returned to Ayrshire to look after her. After her death he returned to Oxford and finished by taking a Third Class Honours degree.

In 1895 he went to live in London and became involved in free-lance journalism. He also published some popular fiction under a pseudonym. In June 1900 he finished the first draft of his study of Gourlay and those to whom he showed it were so impressed that they urged him to expand it into a novel. He lived alone in a cottage in Surrey while writing the book, which was published in 1901 and received on the whole with praise. In the last year of his life he began a second novel which was to be a love story set in Cromwell's time, and made plans for a third novel. As well as this, he made preparations for his marriage to Lizzie MacLennan, the sister of a girl with whom he had been in love and whom he had lost to another man. After a visit to the MacLennans in Glasgow, he was on his way south when he began to feel unwell. For two weeks he struggled on his own against his illness, which was probably pneumonia, but eventually died at Highgate in London on 28 August 1902. He was thirty-three years old.

Do the events of his life illuminate his masterpiece *The House with the Green Shutters*? They do on various levels.

First of all, it is generally agreed that Barbie is modelled on Ochiltree, and there is reason to believe that a house called Kelburn standing by itself on a commanding site half-way down the brae at Ochiltree may have been the model for the House with the Green Shutters. Not all the physical locations fit but it could be that Skeighan corresponds to Cumnock, and Fechars to Kilmarnock.

Secondly, while young Gourlay does not correspond to George Douglas Brown, since one was a successful academic while the other was not, we can surely assume that Brown used some of his own university experience in the book: that he did meet people with the superficial cleverness of the students described; that perhaps he did come across a professor such as the one who read young Gourlay's essay and that students did behave as raucously as they do in the novel.

Then again there was clearly a strong relationship between George Douglas Brown and his mother, the more so as she came from a class inferior to that of his father. The situation again is not exactly the same in the book but there is certainly a close mother-son relationship depicted there.

In relation to the novel, it is no accident that Brown's main study was Classics. If we read Greek tragedies, either in the original or in translation, we find ourselves in the same atmosphere of unrelenting destiny and terror. Event succeeds event, and creates an inflexible mesh from which the hero cannot escape. The hero suffers from *hubris* - or overweening pride — as Gourlay does. On the other hand, it seems as if he cannot do other than he does. Gourlay is a gigantic figure built on the heroic scale, like the Greek hero Ajax, powerful but inarticulate. Also in the Greek tragedies there is a chorus, that is to say, a number of average people who comment on the action and speak for us, the average spectators. They represent very often the voice of reason and caution, as great houses topple, as fate works itself out. George Douglas Brown's innovation is to make this chorus, the 'bodies', small-town people such as the Deacon and the Provost, partial instruments of Gourlay's fall. Unlike members of the Greek chorus, who try to see both sides of the question, they are actively hostile to the hero; they will his destruction and conspire in it. They are like rats snapping at the heels of a large, inarticulate dog. They are also without exception despicable and merciless, and in comparison with them, Gourlay, even with all his weaknesses, seems noble.

CHARACTERISATION

(a) The Gourlays

John Gourlay is the 'hero' of the book. He is arrogant, brutal, insensitive; and yet there are certain qualifications to be made. We are told that he loves his daughter Janet and will sometimes feed her rabbits for her; he shows compassion for his horse and some, too, for Riney, his old servant. In general, however, he treats his employees harshly, he has little time for his son, and he despises his wife and on one occasion hits her so badly that she develops what appears to be breast cancer.

He is a power-seeker as far as his business is concerned, not tolerating any rivals till Wilson out-manoeuvres him. He is at first the only carrier in the town and treats his customers in a cavalier manner. He is not intelligent enough to move with the times or take advantage of change as Wilson does. He has no sense of community, though we must remember that Barbie is a flawed community, lacking leadership both from the minister and the schoolmaster. Gourlay makes enemies easily and often without adequate reason. His contempt for Wilson causes the tragedy which he brings on himself. He has no gift for speech and is in many ways inarticulate. This poses a problem for the author: how do you show the reactions of an inarticulate man to the events around him? For Gourlay has few ideas and no apparent interests apart from his house and business. The author frequently portrays Gourlay's reactions in physical terms. Thus at a crucial moment he breaks his stick in two; at another he hits his wife; at yet another he throws Gibson through a window.

> Gourlay gave no sign. Others would have shown by the moist glisten of self-pity in the eye, or the scowl of wrath, how much they were moved; but Gourlay stared calmly before him, his chin resting on the head of his staff, resolute, immobile, like a stone head at gaze in the desert. Only the larger fulness of his fine nostril betrayed the hell of wrath seething within him. And when they alighted in Skeighan an observant boy said to his mother, 'I saw the marks of his chirted teeth through his jaw.' (p. 138)

His weapon against the 'bodies' is the House with the Green Shutters. It doesn't matter whether he is inarticulate or not, so long as the House stands in its prominent position asserting his riches and the power of his personality. His last action is to try and improve the house. One of the reasons that he cannot stand his wife is that she is not worthy of the House: where he is tidy she is untidy, a slattern. He is, of course, also a very brave man. The description of the night of storm and lightning on which his son was born shows this clearly; it also shows his vanity and wilfulness, which take precedence over his wife's health. There is no-one in Barbie who can stand up to him physically and he is frightened of no man.

Thus he has good qualities as well as bad. However, as happens with the heroes in Greek tragedies, he brings down on himself his own fate or *nemesis*. His pride is too great, his contempt for others too overwhelming. His tragedy is created by his own character. What his wife has become, what his son is, are to a large extent his fault. His son imitates his weaknesses without having any of his good qualities. He is a curiously distorted reflection of his father.

As in all tragedies we feel at the end, 'What a waste!' If only he could have harnessed his courage, his ambition, to better purposes, what a power he might have been. In fact, like a colossal statue, he is pulled down by men who are in many ways smaller than himself. We feel for him a certain pity but at the same time cannot help believing that in his wilful blindness he was the ultimate cause of his own downfall.

Mrs Gourlay is a tragic, ineffectual figure. We are told that in her youth she was an averagely happy girl; we get the impression that Gourlay married her for her money. Now she lavishes her thwarted love on her son and protects him in his weaknesses against his father. She does not ask whether her son is at fault in his treatment of Gilmour; she immediately springs to his defence. She pretends to him that there is nothing wrong with her when in fact she has a fatal disease. She is slovenly, untidy, messy; she is not like the proper mistress of a big house. She is a dreamer and reader of romantic novels. Again, this seems to have a certain inevitability. Since her husband shows no love for her, she has to find her life, meagre as it is, elsewhere and it seems natural enough that she should read such books and love her son in spite of his faults. She is deliberately contrasted with Mrs Wilson who is large, jovial, practical, shrewd and a constant help to her husband. Mrs Gourlay, however, has to put up with continual sarcasm and even violence. She is a pathetic figure, exerting no power, married to a domineering, power-seeking man.

It is only at the end of the book that she shows some strength of character, though perhaps in her concealment of her illness she has shown some earlier. It is she who reveals a final desperate courage in instigating the suicide of herself and her daughter: ' "Gourlay's dochter may gang on the parish if she likes, but his wife never will. *You* may hoast yourself to death in a garret in the poorhouse, but *I'll* follow my boy" ' (p. 243).

Of course, in this novel we are in a hard masculine world. There are women in the novel, some influential, but the atmosphere is male. It is about a projection of the will. In such a world a Mrs Wilson will prevail, but a Mrs Gourlay will go under. There is little tenderness in the book though perhaps her love for her son, doomed though it is, provides some of that tenderness.

Young John Gourlay seems to be exactly the sort of son we would expect such a father and mother to have. He lives under the shadow of his father, who is overwhelmingly physical and powerful, and he is spoiled by his mother. It is perhaps inevitable that he should escape into a dream world of his own. The flaws in his character are many. First of all, he is a coward, and this is often shown throughout the book. He cannot stand up to the other boys in the school; in the scene with the baker at the station he is shown as frightened of the storm; in the closing section of the book he runs away from his father. Secondly, because he is weak, he shelters behind others and bullies them when he can. He uses the power of his father to threaten others, for example, Gilmour, and when he plays truant from school he threatens his sister because she is weaker than he is. He is stupid, bottom of the class where young Wilson is top. He hates both school and university; he fears the unfamiliar and clings to the familiar. He is easily led; he drinks, smokes and plays truant. He will accept responsibility for nothing and when he is caught by the lecturer he refuses to apologise.

Like his father, he is inarticulate but finds a remedy for this in drink. He discovers that by drinking he becomes more sure of himself, and seems also to achieve wit. Thus drink takes over from his mother's love when he is away from her. Where she has her novels, he has his whisky. He is easy prey to the 'bodies' just as his father is, but without his father's indomitable courage. He is boastful, arrogant, silly, and is made a fool of.

He has one gift which is on the whole a weakness. This is his gift of 'sensory perceptiveness' which the author stresses throughout the book. This gift makes him vulnerable to the rawness and brutality of the world but it also enables him to win the Raeburn, an achievement which becomes his ruin. It is quite clear that he is not suited to the academic world. In that sense he is the victim of his father's ambition. He does not have the necessary capacity for work, nor does he have the power of mind. His gift is for the passive imagination, not for the active male energy which his father has. He, like his mother, cannot survive in the harsh world of Barbie.

He is contrasted with young Wilson throughout. Where the latter is cautious, he is wasteful and arrogant; where the latter is hard-working, he is feckless. The very first glimpse we have of young Wilson is of a hard grafter helping his father; young Gourlay, however, does nothing for his father. He is cowardly, bullying, vindictive, boastful, stupid; he has no virtues that one can think of. Yet in a sense he becomes what he has become because of his father and mother. It is hard to blame him since his personality is a pale reflection of theirs. He has inherited the weaknesses of both his parents without any of their virtues. The instrument of his father's death, he disintegrates thereafter and it is no surprise that he commits suicide at the end of the book.

Janet Gourlay is a shadowy figure. She is said to be cleverer than her brother, but suffers from the fatal disease of tuberculosis. She is loved by her father but not so much by her mother who complains that she does not help her as much as she should. At the end of the book she is continually frightened and goes to her death in fear. Little can be said of her, since we are told little. She is a passive victim throughout.

(b) The Wilsons

James Wilson is the instrument of Gourlay's destruction. He has come back to Barbie after marrying and making some money in Aberdeen. He has a fair amount of capital — five hundred pounds — to invest in business. When they first meet in the book, Gourlay quite gratuitously insults him, and by this insult brings about his own financial ruin.

Wilson is a very different kind of man from Gourlay. He is a born businessman, continually thinking of new ways of making money and extending his empire. In a short while, on the assumption that it is better to proceed cautiously and make a small profit on many items, he has seized many opportunities: offering hire purchase terms, working for other merchants, undercutting Gourlay's prices. He also has a helpful wife and son. Wilson, unlike Gourlay, can quickly see, and seize on, the main chance. Thus he instantly realises the vital importance of the railway and makes sure that it passes through Barbie Valley. At the meeting called to discuss the railway, he manoeuvres Gourlay into opposition. Unlike Gourlay, who remains in proud isolation, Wilson uses other people, and makes an ally of the scheming Gibson. He is a good psychologist, as a businessman has to be, and knows who will be useful to him.

Gibson has devised a complex scheme in order to sink Gourlay once and for all. As soon as Gibson points out to him the possibilities, Wilson is quick to see all the ramifications. Together they will destroy Gourlay and together they do so. It is rather ironic that Wilson should be attracted to the scheme partly by the vision of himself as a 'wealthy house-owner' (p. 123). The difference, however, is that Wilson always proceeds in a cautious manner, making sure that he is secure before taking the next step. He has seen what Barbie requires; he provides it and he takes account of his customers.

It is quite clear that Gourlay is no match for Wilson: where Gourlay is interested in 'show', Wilson is a secretive worker behind the scenes; where Gourlay retains his splendid isolation, Wilson manipulates people; where Gourlay rests on his laurels, Wilson is essentially flexible and creative and persistent. And Gourlay has brought this man's emnity down on himself. It is his stupid pride that makes a permanent and relentless foe of a man infinitely more subtle than himself. It is the arrival of Wilson in Barbie that initiates Gourlay's downfall.

Mrs Wilson does not have a major part to play. She is rather seen as a contrast to Mrs Gourlay and as a shrewd, efficient woman. She is gregarious and quick-witted. She deals with the Deacon in a manner calculated to make him look ridiculous: 'and she lifted him out by the scruff of his neck, crying, "Run, mousie, or I'll catch ye!" ' (p. 97). She recognises the cleverness of Gibson and warns her husband about him although he does not need warning. Altogether she is well equipped to survive in the world of Barbie and to be the perfect wife for such a businessman as Wilson is.

Young James Wilson is the sort of son one might expect his parents to have, as young Gourlay is seen to be the inevitable offspring of his. When we meet him first, he is shown to be busy and hard working:

> He was so eager at his work that his clumsy-looking boots – they only *looked* clumsy because the legs they were stuck to were so

> thin — skidded on the cobbles as he whipped round the barn with a chair inverted on his poll. (p. 90)

And later on:
> She had a lass to help her in the house now, and the red-headed boy was always to be seen, jinking round corners like a weasel, running messages hot-foot, errand boy to the 'bisness' in general.
> (p. 103)

He seems to be continually in motion, and clever at school. His letter home after visiting Jock Allan is worth examining for its malignity and its concern with money: we can see that he will turn out like his father, clever, hard-working, prudent, a complete contrast to the wasteful young Gourlay. His cleverness, however, has its part to play in precipitating the tragedy since it leads to Gourlay's decision to send his own son to university and to the disastrous events which follow.

There are a number of other characters who may appear to be minor but are important in giving depth and variety to the book.

(c) Minor Characters

The other characters in the book can be briefly disposed of. Jock Allan and his coterie are instrumental in the fall of young Gourlay while also providing a certain intellectual background which the book conspicuously lacks, for the two ministers and the schoolmaster are immersed in their own concerns. Gibson is the personification of the ruthless, cunning 'ethic' of business. Templandmuir, earlier manipulated by Gourlay, asserts himself at a crucial point and Riney personifies the doggedly loyal worker.

The '**bodies**' are shown as persistently hostile to the hero, apart from Coe and the baker; the baker revealing a degree of humanity which helps to balance, however minimally, the general blackness of the book. They are well differentiated. The Deacon has his lisp; Sandy Toddle has his 'posh' way of speaking; the Provost is pompous and rather stupid; Tam Brodie is sharp and is one of the first to appreciate Wilson as a business man; the baker who quotes Burns is humane and fair; Tam Wylie is clever and wealthy although he pretends to be poor; Coe tries to defend Gourlay at times and it is he who tells the story of Gourlay's courage in the storm. The Deacon seems to be the leader. It is he who is elected by the others to speak to

Gourlay about the water supply 'for the common good'. He is an expert in probing for the weakest point in a man's armour, clever, quick and able to vary his tactics, as, for instance, when he flatters young Gourlay. In his own way he is a man of great ability though that ability is put to bad use. The baker at one point calls him 'an artist in spite'. The Deacon and most of the others use language to destroy the inarticulate Gourlay. We feel, however, that even Gourlay is preferable to the cowardly 'bodies' who will his destruction and conspire in it.

STRUCTURE

The structure of the novel is in three parts. Chapters One to Eight show Gourlay at his most prosperous. Chapters Nine to Fifteen introduce Wilson and describe his methods of starting and expanding his business and undermining Gourlay's. Chapter Sixteen to the end of the book shows Gourlay's decision to send his son to University and the tough consequences of this decision. Let us look at these sections in detail.

(a) Prosperity

In the first section, covering one day, we see Gourlay as the apparent master of all he surveys. He dominates his surroundings, his servants, his wife and son. His house is the best in the town and he is continually making improvements to it. His carts set out, each horse matched for colour with its neighbour. The 'bodies' may insult him behind his back but at this stage he appears invulnerable. We see him happy in his possessions and easy power:

> He was delighting in the sense of his own property around him, the most substantial pleasure possible to man. His feeling, deep though it was, was quite vague and inarticulate. If you had asked Gourlay what he was thinking of he could not have told you, even if he had been willing to answer you civilly — which is most unlikely. Yet his whole being, physical and mental (physical, indeed, rather than mental), was surcharged with the feeling that the fine buildings around him were his, that he had won them by his own effort and built them large and significant before the world. He was lapped in the thought of it.   (p. 48)

Yet in spite of this outward tranquillity we sense that there are forces moving below it which can be inimical to his prosperity. There is first of all his wife, who is untidy and slatternly and not suited to the splendid house. There is the son who is cowardly and bullying. There are the 'bodies' who are viciously hostile. There is the quarrel with Gilmour. There is the sense of a man who will not under any circumstances compromise, as is shown by his attitude towards the community in the incident of the water. We also see that he is dependent on Templandmuir. So there are hints of vulnerability beneath the splendid facade.

THE HOUSE WITH THE GREEN SHUTTERS 17

(b) Decline

The second section introduces Wilson who will destroy Gourlay. It is typical of Gourlay's dour stupidity that he antagonises Wilson needlessly, and makes a permanent and inveterate enemy of a man who is better at business than he is himself. Wilson comes to Barbie and immediately sets out, little by little, to create his own business, firstly his Emporium, and then his wider trade which will encroach on Gourlay's. He shows an appreciation of his customers; he uses posters to advertise; he introduces hire purchase; he sees the advantages of the railway; he becomes a leader in the community. He is articulate where Gourlay is not; he makes friends of people instead of enemies; he has a wife and son who help him with his business; he does not become obsessed with property nor are his business premises even tidy. Along with Gibson, he concocts a scheme which will destroy Gourlay. Templandmuir also withdraws his support for Gourlay by taking back the lease of the quarry. We see Gourlay's troubles multiplying as he is outwitted again and again by a rival who is a natural businessman and one who can foresee the direction of the forces of change and how he can best make use of them. Gourlay involves himself in an expensive law suit with Gibson. Financially, he is beginning to feel the strain:

> Gourlay was hard up for money. Every day of his life taught him that he was nowhere in the stress of modern competition. The grand days — only a few years back, but seeming half a century away, so much had happened in between — the grand days when he was the only big man in the locality, and carried everything with a high hand, had disappeared for ever. Now all was bustle, hurry, and confusion, the getting and sending of telegrams, quick despatches by railway, the watching of markets at a distance, rapid combinations that bewildered Gourlay's duller mind. At first he was too obstinate to try the newer methods; when he did he was too stupid to use them cleverly. (p. 135)

He has to borrow against the security of the House with the Green Shutters. And then he makes another mistake. Simply out of rivalry with Wilson he sends his son to University.

(c) Tragic Outcome

The third section highlights young Gourlay's character and failure at the university. We can see, even from the earlier passages in the book, that young Gourlay is not suited to academic learning. He was never happy at school and played truant. When he goes to Edinburgh he misses Barbie since he has never been out in the wide world before. In order to ease his entry into a society cleverer than the one he has been used to, he takes to drink. Then, strangely enough, he has a major success, which is the winning of the Raeburn Prize. But this triumph, which his father enjoys, is his ultimate downfall. It makes him believe that he is cleverer than he really is. Instead of spurring him on to harder work, it makes him even more idle than he was before. He shows off, he drinks heavily. He has a confrontation with a lecturer and is sent home in disgrace. Now Gourlay is besieged by failure on all sides. His wife is ill and it was he who caused her illness by hitting her. His son is a drunkard and a failure; there is danger of losing the House with the Green Shutters; his business is in ruins. He has a quarrel with his son in which his son kills him. His son has nightmares of his father's eyes following him everywhere and drinks even more heavily than before. A letter arrives from the lawyers stating that the mortgage payments on the house are behind. Young Gourlay commits suicide, and so finally do his mother and sister. The House with the Green Shutters contains three dead bodies. Gourlay's world has fallen.

We can see, therefore, the remorseless progress of the plot. One event leads to another in a dreadful chain. First the limelight falls on Gourlay, then on Wilson, then on Gourlay's son. Every event seems to generate its own inevitable result. Gourlay's mockery of Wilson creates its own consequences; the unfitness of Gourlay's son for university creates its consequences.

OTHER STRUCTURAL FEATURES

(a) Parallelism

The author introduces into the story deliberate parallels. Thus, for instance, we can compare the story of young Gourlay's birth accompanied by thunder and lightning to the scene where young Gourlay meets the baker at the station. A number of things are going on in the latter scene. First of all, it shows a deliberate contrast between young Gourlay and his father: where the father was brave, the son is cowardly. But there is more to it than that. While also showing young Gourlay's imagination — which is the source of his cowardice — it also refers to an 'eye'. Afterwards the 'eye' becomes the 'eyes' that follow young Gourlay after the death of his father: ' "The heavens are opening and shutting like a man's eye," said Gourlay; "oh, it's a terrible thing the world — " and he covered his face with his hands' (p. 131).

Then as we read the book carefully we notice that the 'slovenly' chambermaid at the beginning of the novel is the precursor of the slovenly Mrs Gourlay; that Gourlay's house contrasts favourably with Wilson's; that the incident with the poker (p. 83) is intended to prepare us for the murder at the end of the book; that an earlier outwitting of Gourlay by Gibson makes the latter's brilliant plan more believable; that Gourlay's attitude of 'take it or leave it' to his customers is deliberately contrasted with Wilson's obsequious advertisements in which he says: 'Moreover, to meet the convenience of his customers, J.W. will deliver goods at your own doors' (p. 92).

(b) Recurring Images

Finally, certain images appear again and again throughout the book. Thus, for instance, there is the image of the 'eye' which is prepared for long before the nightmarish experiences of young Gourlay at the end:

> . . . a black gleam shot from his eye (p. 40)
>
> 'He has the black glower in his e'en.' (p. 41)
>
> Gilmour shrank from the blaze in his eyes. (p. 58)
>
> Or if you did venture a bit jibe when you met him, he glowered you off the face of the earth with thae black e'en of his. (p. 65)

In this book the eye is used as an instrument of power, of intimidation. Gourlay, inexpert in speech, glowers at people to cow them. And furthermore in a small town like Barbie all is open to the eye. One is watched all the time.

Another feature of the novel is the strong use the author makes of colours. One in particular, yellow, stands out.

> The hands of the clock across 'the Square' were pointing to the hour of eight. They were yellow in the sun. (p. 39)
>
> The sun streamed through the window in yellow heat right on to a pat of melting butter. (p. 52)
>
> 'Whose yellow doag's that?' (p. 61)
>
> . . . and now the light lay, yellow and vivid, on a red clinker of coal . . .   (p. 82)
>
> The stranger wore a light yellow overcoat . . .   (p. 86)

> There it [i.e. the barn] remains and gives a ripeness to the place, matching fitly with the great horse-chestnut yellowing before the door ... (p. 95)
>
> Behind the other counter were canisters in goodly rows, barrels of flour and bags of meal, and great yellow cheeses in the window. (p. 96)
>
> The leaves of a Bible fluttered in the fresh wind from the door. A large lamp was burning on the table. Its big yellow flame was unnatural in the sunshine. (p. 246)

These unitary images of colour — and the references to 'eyes' — are like themes in music which give a density to the book.

The manner, then, in which the author has structured the plot emphasises the tragic inevitability of Gourlay's fall. And as in Greek tragedy we have a houseful of deaths at the end, so here we have the same. It is fitting also that, since the book is entitled *The House with the Green Shutters*, the last sentence in the book should be about it: 'They gazed with blanched faces at the House with the Green Shutters, sitting dark there and terrible, beneath the radiant arch of the dawn' (p. 247). And it is also fitting that the 'radiant arch' duplicates the very beginning of the book where the 'smooth round arch of the falling water glistened for a moment in mid-air' (p. 39).

LANGUAGE

(a) Style

One of the most important aspects of the author's style is his visual power. The author sees what he is writing about, whether places or people, very clearly and, therefore, the reader sees them clearly.

The opening of the book has this extraordinary visual quality:

> The freshness of the air, the smoke rising thin and far above the red chimneys, the sunshine glistering on the roofs and gables, the rosy clearness of everything beneath the dawn, above all the quietness and peace, made Barbie, usually so poor to see, a very pleasant place to look down at on a summer morning. (p. 39)

This clarity is also seen in the description of the kitchen:

> As Gourlay shoved his feet into his boots, and stamped to make them easy, he glowered at the kitchen from under his heavy brows with a huge disgust. The table was littered with unwashed dishes, and on the corner of it next him was a great black sloppy ring, showing where a wet saucepan had been laid upon the bare board. The sun streamed through the window in yellow heat right on to a pat of melting butter. (p. 52)

We can tell immediately from this description of the kitchen what Mrs Gourlay is like, that she is slovenly, untidy, neglectful. In that sense the author sometimes uses descriptions of physical objects as a substitute for description of character. He describes Gibson as:

> a man with mean brown eyes. Brown eyes may be clear and limpid as a mountain pool, or they may have the fine black flash of anger and the jovial gleam, or they may be mean things — little and sly and oily. Gibson's had the depth of cunning, not the depth of character, and they glistened like the eyes of a lustful animal. He was a reddish man, with a fringe of sandy beard, and a perpetual grin which showed his yellow teeth, with green deposit round their roots ... He was not florid, yet that grin of his seemed to intensify his reddishness ... so that the baker christened him long ago 'the man with the sandy smile'. (p. 118)

Even relatively minor characters like the Rev. Mr Struthers are described in the same meticulous manner:

> He had big splay feet, short stout legs, and a body of such bulging bulbosity, that all the droppings of his spoon — which were many — were caught on the round of his black waistcoat, which always looked as if it had been newly spattered by a grey shower. His eye-brows were bushy and white, and the hairs slanting up and out rendered the meagre brow even narrower than it was. His complexion, more especially in cold weather, was a dark crimson. The purply colour of his face was intensified by the pure whiteness of the side whiskers projecting stiffly by his ears, and in mid-week, when he was unshaven, his redness revealed more plainly, in turn, the short gleaming stubble that lay like rime upon his chin. (p. 172)

Thus we can see the intense focus which the author applies both to people and to material objects.

The book is not one of abstract ideas and thus it is natural that there should be a strong physical dimension, reinforced throughout by physical, almost muscular, gestures and reactions attributed not only to Gourlay but also to other characters. Of Gilmour he writes: ' ... his master smiled grimly at the sudden redness that swelled his neck and ears to the verge of bursting' (p. 47). And of Mrs Gourlay: ' "Ye muckle lump!" she cried shrilly, the two scraggy muscles of her neck standing out long and thin as she screamed; "ye muckle lump — to strike a defenceless wean!" ' (p. 57). Later he describes how Gourlay 'struck the door with his clenched fist till the blood streamed on his knuckles' (p. 115).

There are strong physical verbs throughout, describing confrontations of various kinds: fists, eyes, faces, are important, so also are objects like the house itself, and the stick which Gourlay breaks. There is so much violence and argument in the book, including Gourlay's attack on his wife and on Gibson and his fierce confrontation with his son at the end.

It is only at the conclusion of the novel that the writer loses his precise visual and physical control, and the language becomes melodramatic and unfocussed. As the house falls apart, so also does the language:

> 'I have killed my faither,' he said slowly, pausing long between every phrase: 'I have killed my faither ... I have killed my faither. And he's foll-owing me, ... he's foll-owing me ... he's

> foll-owing me.' It was the voice of a thing, not a man. (p. 235)

> 'Oh, my poor, poor mother!' cried Janet with a bursting sob, her eyes raining hot tears. (p. 242)

> Suddenly Mrs Gourlay screamed with wild laughter, and, laughing, eyed with mirthless merriment, the look of horror with which Janet was regarding her. 'Ha, ha, ha!' she screamed, 'it's to be a clean sweep o' the Gourlays! Ha, ha, ha! it's to be a clean sweep o' the Gourlays!' (p. 243)

It is interesting to see how repetitive and banal the language becomes at this point in the book.

The difficulty that the author had here was that, although he modelled his book on the fall of a great Greek house in a tragedy, the characters who inhabit this house are unremarkable and have no profound statements to make about life, since they represent nothing but themselves and their fall is in a sense unrepresentative. Thus the poor quality of the characters' minds makes the author skate closely to the world of sentiment and broken language. He has to pay at the end for the ordinariness of Mrs Gourlay and her daughter and son.

For much of the book, however, the stylistic control is consummate. And if we want to see that style at its best it must surely be in Chapter 22, when Gourlay dismisses Riney. This is great writing, achieved apparently effortlessly. But we should notice the physical details which contribute to it: 'Peter rose stiffly from his knees and shook the mould with a pitiful gesture from his hands. His mouth had fallen slack, and showed a few yellow tusks' (p. 187). And later: 'Peter said nothing, but gazed away down the garden, his sunken mouth forgetting to munch its straw, which dangled by his chin' (p. 187). It is a beautiful, moving moment, close to tears, and shows the author's style at its best.

(b) Scots — English

The author uses English for narration and descriptions of places and people, and Scots for dialogue. The Gourlays and the 'bodies' speak Scots. As used by them, it is the language of conversation and of insult. English is used for business transactions and education. Wilson feels he must use English to further his business and David Aird uses English to show contempt for his origins.

The Scots spoken by Gourlay and the 'bodies' has a cruel intimacy that English lacks. In the confrontation between Wilson and Gourlay, on their first meeting when Wilson is trying to achieve some intimacy with Gourlay, the latter cuts him down to size with his brutal remarks: ' "Oh, auld Wilson, the mole-catcher!" said contemptuous Gourlay. "What's this they christened him now? 'Toddling Johnnie', was it noat?" ' (p. 87).

In the last moving scene in the novel, the departure of Peter Riney, Scots is used to fine effect. Here we have the loyal Scottish values of the past encapsulated in brief Scots phrases which are very moving. It is as if a farewell is being said from the 'new' world not just to Peter Riney, but to all the Peter Rineys of that era: ' "I'm gey auld," said Peter, still shaking his hands with that pitiful gesture, 'but I only need a bite and a sup. Man, I'm willin' to tak onything" ' (p. 187). The two are face to face as human beings transcending even rank, as is shown by the use of the word 'man'. The scene trembles between the spoken and the unspoken, at last arriving at Peter's final sad statement: "I'll feenish the tatties at ony rate" ' (p. 187).

The young boys at school speak Scots. Swipey taunts young Gourlay with the remark: ' "Come on, Gourlay, ... and I'll poultice the road wi' your brose" ' (p. 78), and earlier Gourlay repeats word for word what his father has said to Gilmour: ' "Man, I could kill ye wi' a glower!" ' (p. 77).

The group of students surrounding Jock Allan speak a kind of affected English; nevertheless they take pleasure in referring to the greater succinctness of Scots as against English, illustrated by a story in which a Scot calls 'incense' a 'burning stink'.

The novel portrays a society beginning to change, and Wilson's use of language reflects this. He tends to speak English rather than Scots:

> 'Oh,' said Wilson, getting in a fine one at Gourlay, 'there's no drawback in that! The ways o' business have changed greatly since steam came close to our doors. It's nothing but vanity nowadays when a country merchant wastes money on a ramshackle of buildings for storing — there's no need for that if he only had brains to develop quick deliveries.' (p. 104)

And he uses English quite deliberately in his advertisement with its oily obsequiousness:

> Mr James Wilson begs to announce to the inhabitants of Barbie and surrounding neighbourhood that he has taken these commodious premises, No. 1, The Cross, which he intends to open shortly as a Grocery, Ironmongery and General Provision Store.

> J.W. is apprised that such an Emporium has long been a felt want in the locality. (p. 92)

It is interesting that at a certain point Wilson uses his initials as if to import into the long-winded English a false intimacy with his intended public. The whole advertisement is worth examining in detail, for it shows quite clearly that the author knows exactly what he is doing in his use of language. Throughout the novel a controlled, exact, English narrative style is set against the quick, lively and often poisonous Scots.

Wilson's use of English shows most clearly the new world of commerce which will destroy the older Scottish world in which Gourlay prospered. Templandmuir, though not invariably, speaks English rather than Scots: ' "I don't follow Mr Gourlay at all," he roared. "I follow nobody but myself! Every man in the district's in support of this petition. It would be absurd to suppose anything else" ' (p. 114). The Rev. Mr Struthers congratulates young Gourlay for his success in the Raeburn Essay in English. David Aird attempts an affected style of English which he considers fashionable: ' " . . . just down for a flying visit to see my little girl. Dem'd glad to get back to town again" ' (p. 184). Mrs Gourlay reads English romantic novels whose language completely lacks the vivid immediacy of the author's own prose in English and certainly lacks the abrupt intimacy of the Scots.

English is increasingly the language of rank, educational success and commerce. Barbie is a changing community, not only economically but linguistically. It is part of Gourlay's tragedy that there is no place for him in this 'brave new world'.

AN ESTIMATE OF THE NOVEL

When assessing *The House with the Green Shutters* as a novel, we cannot avoid mentioning the Kailyard School. This is in essence a contemptuous name given to a number of writers who wrote in Scotland at the end of the nineteenth and beginning of the twentieth centuries.

In general, the Kailyard School is considered to be sentimental, rural, nostalgic, avoiding great social issues, cosy. One of its themes is that of the lad who makes good by means of education. It is only fair to say that recent revaluations suggest that there is a real power of observation among the Kailyard novels and that in a sense they were a picture of a real though limited Scotland.

However, when we consider *The House with the Green Shutters* we see that it is much harsher, much more raw and unsparing in its attitude to some of its characters than the writings of the Kailyard School were. On the other hand, we should note what the author himself wrote to an old acquaintance in Ochiltree:

> Dear Mrs. Watson,
>   I thank you very much for the kindly letter you sent me, and am glad to have your father's verses. I am afraid, however, you will be sadly disappointed by "The House with the Green Shutters". It is anything but a kindly book. Yet it was written with a kindly enough intention. I hate scandal, malevolence, and all manner of cruelty; and in this book I tried to hold them up to scorn and loathing ... [1]

He was also to comment that his book was

> more complimentary to Scotland, I think, than the sentimental slop of Barrie, and Crockett, and Maclaren. It was antagonism to their method that made me embitter the blackness. ... Which was a gross blunder, of course. A novelist should never have an axe of his own to grind. If he allows a personal animus to obtrude ever so slightly it knocks his work out of balance. He should be an aloof individual, if possible, stating all sides and taking none.[2]

It could be said, therefore, that the blackness of the novel is as false to small-town life in Scotland as the 'rosiness' of the Kailyard School was. Yet what is unarguably true is that he had

THE HOUSE WITH THE GREEN SHUTTERS

the same material to work on as the Kailyard School had. There is the minister, the schoolmaster, the scholar who tries to make good. However, neither the minister nor the schoolmaster in this book is interested in the community.

An atmosphere of blackness pervades the whole book. Relationships between husband and wife, between father and son, are black; communal relationships seem to be non-existent; there is drunkenness and violence; there is a hunger for advancement and money, and there is pride. The question is, what sort of balance of 'goodness' is available? In fact, there does not appear to be much. There is the loyalty of Peter Riney, the kindness of the baker and Coe, but there does not appear to be much else. There is little natural affection. Sometimes we get the impression that the author himself hates the characters. There is not much humour either — and what there is is of a dark, sadistic kind.

What we get is a certain truth, but on the whole it is a one-sided truth. We cannot imagine a community quite so venomous, quite without redeeming features. It is possible, of course, that there was a lot for the author to remember with malice. There was the stigma of his illegitimate birth, for instance, and his unhappiness at Oxford. On the other hand, there seems to be evidence that the novelist 'could be a friendly cheerful person, ready to relax and enjoy a joke or chat.'[3] Whatever the truth of this, there is no doubt that the novel is a dark one. There is no sign, for instance, of a belief in God by the author himself, which might have been a balancing factor. And, as has already been remarked, the comfort which should have come from the minister is absent. True, at the end of the book there is a reference to the Bible but it is almost certainly ironical.

My own feeling is that behind the book is the Darwinian theory of the survival of the fittest. It is almost as if the 'bodies' were little animals hunting down a bigger animal. If we examine the book, we find more references to animals than would appear by chance. I am not referring here to Janet's rabbits or her father's pony, or the fact that Gourlay seemed to be happier with languageless animals than with people, but to the author's use of animals as metaphors, men being compared to animals. Thus there are references to 'Simpson, the swine!' (p. 42); 'demned ess' (p. 46), 'a muckle sheep' (p. 51); 'Run, mousie, or I'll catch ye!' (p. 97), 'jinking round corners like a weasel' (p. 103). Gourlay is compared to a donkey (p. 45). The meeting called to discuss the implications of the railway is compared to a 'cellarful of snakes' (p. 114). These are only a few of the references to the animal world; within the book there is a whole zoo of animals mentioned — mice, rats, dogs, cockerels, tigers, weasels, wolves, chickens, sheep, lambs, kittens, bulls, and so on.

The book gives the impression of being set in an animal world without charity. Gourlay himself appears like a bewildered bull being maddened by stinging insects. He has the inarticulacy of the animal. People prey on each other as Gibson and Wilson do on Gourlay. It is a closed, terrible world, aggressive and treacherous, certainly not 'rose-coloured'. The Christian goodness which might have corrected the balance a little is absent. What then of education which might also have acted as a potential balancing force?

Let us examine the place of education in this book. There is little sense of education as an end in itself; education seems to be a method of gaining power. And even the novels Mrs Gourlay reads are a poor substitute for the reality of good books; they represent an escape from the real world, not a method of coping with it.

Again, to young Gourlay his first school was 'a howling wilderness' (p. 75). The cut that he got over his 'cowering shoulders' (p. 76) for being late suggests that his teacher was one of the traditional Scottish kind, instilling education by fear, and this impression we get of the schoolmaster is reinforced later when young Gourlay is hiding in the garret: 'Things of the outer world, where he swaggered among his fellows and was thrashed, or bungled his lessons and was thrashed again, imprinted themselves vividly on his mind . . . ' (p. 81).

In this novel, education is a social good; that is to say, it is a means of becoming better than, or at least as good as, your neighbour. Gourlay's motives for sending his son first to Skeighan High School and then to University are not truly educational ones; he is to go to these establishments simply because young Wilson is going. And young Gourlay sees education as a social thing too: 'When he passed his old classmates (apprentice-grocers now and carters and ploughboys) his febrile insolence led him to swagger and assume' (p. 129). Nor is the author much more flattering to young Wilson: 'He was one of the gimlet characters who, by diligence and memory, gain prizes in their schooldays — and are fools for the remainder of their lives' (p. 129).

This is not education seen as an opening of windows or as a blossoming of the imagination. It is a function of the cautious, prudent Scot, who thinks that it is an acquisition that will be useful to him. Young Gourlay often plays truant from both schools he attends. When his father catches him playing truant from the High School, he takes him back to the school, saying to the baker, ' "Me thrash him! . . . I pay the High School of Skeighan to thrash him, and I'll take damned good care I get my money's worth" ' (p. 132). To Gourlay, education is an investment: he expects to get fair returns from it as he would expect from a business. Nor do the students at the university have wide-ranging minds, though they have a certain brittle wit. Thus they approve of 'Bauldy' who called the incense in Notre Dame a 'burning stink'. There is no recognition of Notre Dame as a magnificent cathedral. To a large extent they are products of the system that has produced them. They talk of the Scottish 'peasantry' and admire its narrow sayings. And, of course, this student society is shown as a hard-drinking one.

Professor Tam, too, has a limited view of education: 'He used to lecture on the fifteen characteristics of Lady Macbeth . . . , and he would announce quite gravely, "We will now approach the discussion of the eleventh feature of the lady" ' (p. 160). As for the dramatic Lady Macbeth, she is forgotten in this mathematical skeleton he has made of her. Yet he is shown by the author to be in some ways exceptional. For instance, he gives the Raeburn prize to young Gourlay because he has seen imagination in the essay the latter has handed in.

The Raeburn in its turn is considered by Gourlay senior to be a trophy brought home to confound the Wilsons. It is not considered as an educational triumph for its own sake: ' "Did young Wilson get anything?" came the eager cry' (p. 166).

The education in this book, consequently, is not seen as a liberalising influence; rather it is a function of hard work and memory. It has been converted into a status symbol. It is based on fear rather than encouragement and understanding. It is possible that in a more sympathetic system young Gourlay's fate might have been different.

Since Scottish education concentrated on the memory and on diligence, and taught through fear, there is a lack of feeling among many of the characters in the book. Instead of the 'intellect' we have low cunning, and instead of verbal skill, inarticulacy. Gourlay, himself bred on fear, instils fear in all around him. He never seems to have made any attempt to understand his son. Education is simply another weapon to be used in the armoury of life. The book is a damning indictment of the Scottish educational system (as it used to be) by one who had come through it. It suggests no alternative to a limited Scottish society because it itself is so limited, and indeed it made Scottish society to a great extent what it was. It opens no windows; it is, as has been said, another weapon in the survival of the fittest.

There is one other question that should be considered in relation to this novel: how far was it meant to be a record of social transition?

Certainly there is a sense of social change in the book. There is the coming of the railway and the mines. There is a sense of 'new' men such as Wilson instigating changes in selling techniques, and a greater concentration on modern methods. There is the rise of the 'pure' business mentality, perhaps more ruthless but also more aware of the consumer. Gourlay is left behind by cleverer, more astute men, in short, by better business men.

And yet in no sense is Brown writing a book of social realism except incidentally. The centre of the book, and of Brown's main interest, is first and last Gourlay himself. It is true that Brown is said to have been interested in the French novelist, Honoré Balzac, who set out to create a vast gallery of characters enmeshed in social change. Nevertheless, this actual economic background is, I think, used by Brown to bring Gourlay to his fatal confrontation with Wilson and to his downfall.

In other words, Gourlay need not have been a businessman for his character to have led him to tragedy. For the author's purposes, it is possible to imagine Gourlay as being involved in some other kind of work. We must also remember that Gourlay was probably based on Brown's own father, who was a carter for a while, and also a vitriolic and colourful personality. The novelist uses the material with which he is most familiar.

If we consider Gourlay to be modelled on the classical hero of tragedy, then many of the questions answer themselves. The tragic hero traditionally finds himself involved in circumstances which demand choices from him. These circumstances are such as will test his weakness. Gourlay's weakness is his pride and the circumstances are designed to test that pride. From the moment that he encounters Wilson, he is forced into making decisions which will ultimately destroy him. His most important decision is to send his son to the High School and then to University in the midst of difficult financial circumstances. Tragedy is the inexorable machine inside which the hero is caught. It is, however, possible to conceive of circumstances which would have brought the same terrible consequences, and, even if this were not the case, it is Gourlay's extraordinary regard for the House with the Green Shutters which is of decisive importance. We always have to remind ourselves that the author chose to call his novel *The House with the Green Shutters*.

Thus it is character rather than circumstances which the author is ultimately concerned with, and with the character of Gourlay especially. It is from him that the novel is generated. In examining other people, we are always driven to scrutinising them in relation to Gourlay. It is his naked will that dominates the book. It is because of him that his wife and son are what they are; it is in relation to him that we see the 'bodies'. He it is who makes an inveterate enemy of Wilson. It is noteworthy that Wilson is at first an admirer of Gourlay and wishes to be accepted by him. It is Gourlay who deliberately punctures that respect.

In fact, it has been suggested that Gourlay represents the tradition of the diabolic in Scottish literature, the recurring use of the Devil as an element in story-telling. There are continual references to Gourlay's black looks, his glower, to the power of his eye. From this point of view he might seem to be like Gil-Martin in James Hogg's *Confessions of a Justified Sinner*, or even like Edward Hyde in Robert Louis Stevenson's *The Strange Case of Dr Jekyll and Mr Hyde*, both characters representing the devilish or darker side of human nature.

My own feeling is that we do not need the idea of the diabolical to interpret Gourlay's character. Though social realism does not explain him, we need not despair. It is a fact that we have in many other tragedies, both Greek and Shakespearean, characters who are possessed by the kind of pride which demands punishment. King Lear is one; Oedipus is another. These people transgress limits which are taken to be human. They therefore bring disaster on themselves.

What is missing from this book is a moral background from which the hero can be seen. After all, who would not dislike the 'bodies' and the world which they represent, even though we have to remember that some of their spite is generated by Gourlay himself? The weakness of the book is that Gourlay is in many ways a heroic figure, but the only one. His wife and children are not. And as well as this, Gourlay's actions do not relate to a higher moral code; at the end they only have to do with himself. Nor, indeed, does he learn from his torments as Lear does. There is no sense in which he learns to know himself better. He goes down but he blames others for his torments.

There is an invincible stupidity in him and there is, therefore, no real illumination at the end of the novel. The material available to Brown is not enough for him to write a great tragedy.

But still this is a most impressive book. It is full of raw power. It is a book that is artistically formed; the author knew exactly what he was doing. He himself is said to have admired books where the characters leap alive and vivid from the page and certainly many of the characters in this book do so. It is concerned with a certain side of Scottish nature and experience: the small-town mentality, demeaning, narrow, diminishing. It is ultimately lacking, perhaps, in the objective purity of great art. However, that it is one of the great novels of the Scottish literary tradition cannot be doubted, nor can it be doubted that Gourlay is one of the great creations of the Scottish novel. His pride is his main characteristic but it is a specifically Scottish pride, pride in possessions, pride in power, pride in male domination. The novel represents the maleness of Scottish society. In both classical and Shakespearean tragedy there have been women of unquestionable force, brilliance or tenderness: Antigone, Lady Macbeth, Cordelia and many others. Here there is the raw, sheer, naked power of Scottish maleness, without insight into the self.

It is true that this is Brown's one major book; he died, as we have seen, at the age of thirty-three. What he might have produced after getting this book out of his system we cannot tell. Whether it would have the same raw power it is hard to know. In some deep sense Brown himself was deeply involved in the book, perhaps more deeply than is usual with authors.

There is a blackness about the book which the author himself recognised, but there is a lot of real, living power too. The book is full of real people, fighting, hating, confronting each other. And they are recognisable. What the novel lacks is love. It may be that there had not been much love in the author's own life. That might have come, and with it a greater book. What we have in the novel is male strength and the drive towards power. What it lacks is feminine gentleness. The terrifying thing is that, given the nature of Scottish society as shown in this novel, there might be a great deal in his insight into a society lacking love and tenderness that remains relevant to Scotland today.

NOTES

1 Ian Campbell, 'George Douglas Brown. A Study in Objectivity' in *Nineteenth-Century Scottish Fiction, a Critical Anthology*, ed. Ian Campbell (Manchester: Carcanet Press, 1979), pp. 142-62 (p. 148).
2 As above, p. 149.
3 George Douglas Brown, *The House with the Green Shutters*, intro. J.T. Low (Edinburgh: Holmes McDougall, 1974), p. xi.

FOR FURTHER STUDY

1. Differentiate carefully among the 'bodies', showing which are hostile to Gourlay and which have some sympathy for him.
2. How far does Gourlay bring his troubles down on himself?
3. What part do women play in the book?
4. What is the difference between Gourlay and Wilson in their attitudes towards business?
5. What do you learn about universities in the days in which this book is set?
6. Do you feel any sympathy at all for Gourlay?
7. Do you feel that Gourlay senior is entirely responsible for what his son has become?
8. If you have any knowledge of small-town life, are you convinced by the portrait of Barbie?
9. If you had lived in Barbie, what do you think your own attitude to Gourlay would have been?
10. Among the Seven Deadly Sins are Pride, Avarice and Envy. How far are they shown in operation in the book?
11. Why do you think the book is called *The House with the Green Shutters* rather than, for instance, *Gourlay*?
12. Study the episode on the gig in Chapter 15. By what methods do the 'bodies' enrage Gourlay?
13. Look at the scene in Chapter 22 in which Gourlay dismisses Peter Riney. How does the author gain his effects?
14. There are certain minor characters in the book, such as Jock Allan, David Aird, the lecturer who reports young Gourlay, the Rev. Mr Struthers. What do you think they contribute to the novel?

BIBLIOGRAPHY

Campbell, Ian, 'George Douglas Brown. A Study in Objectivity' in *Nineteenth-Century Scottish Fiction, a Critical Anthology*, ed. Ian Campbell (Manchester: Carcanet Press, 1979), pp. 148-62.

Lang, Andrew, introduction to Lennox, Cuthbert, *George Douglas Brown* (see below).

Lennox, Cuthbert, *George Douglas Brown* (London: Hodder and Stoughton, 1903).

Low, J.T., introduction to *The House with the Green Shutters* (Edinburgh: Holmes McDougall, 1974).

McClure, J. Derrick, 'Dialect in *The House with the Green Shutters*', *Studies in Scottish Literature*, vol. 9 (1971-2), pp. 148-63.

Melrose, Andrew, 'George Douglas Brown, a Biographical Sketch and an Appreciation' in *The House with the Green Shutters*, Memorial edn (London: Andrew Melrose, 1923).

Melrose, Andrew, 'George Douglas Brown, Reminiscences of a Friendship and a Notable Novel' in Lennox, Cuthbert, *George Douglas Brown* (see above).

Porter, Dorothy, introduction to *The House with the Green Shutters* (Harmondsworth: Penguin Books, 1985).

Smith, Iain Crichton, '*The House with the Green Shutters*', *Studies in Scottish Literature*, vol. 7 (1969-70), pp. 3-10.

Veitch, James, *George Douglas Brown* (London: Herbert Jenkins, 1952).

Audio Cassette Commentaries

Ian Campbell, *'The House with the Green Shutters' (A) Tone.*
Ian Campbell, *'The House with the Green Shutters' (B) Characterisation.*
  These tapes are available from ASLS (see back cover).

GLOSSARY

The aim of this Glossary is to provide a simple guide to the Scots words and phrases found in the book that may not be in common usage. It stands as a safety net for the reader should one day the annotated versions edited by Dr J.T. Low and Dorothy Porter (see Bibliography) become unavailable. Further help can be found in *The Concise Scots Dictionary* (Aberdeen: Aberdeen University Press, 1985).

ablow below
acqueesh between
ae one
ahint behind
aicht eight
aince wud aye waur once mad ever the worse for it
airt direction, path, quarter
aiver cart-horse
atweel indeed, surely
aucht possession
auld wives old women (used of men who are weak and cautious)
auld-farrant old-fashioned
aumous alms, charity

baikie stool
barley-bree whisky
bass door mat
batts colic in horses
bauld daring
bawbee money, small coin
bellman town crier
ben (the hoose) into the next room (in the house)
besom brush; bitchy female
bide stay
bien fine and upstanding
bill bull
billies lads
birkie smart
birr energy
bit little (adj.)
bittock little (noun)

blagyird bad character
bleach beat
bodies folk
brae hillside
branks bridle; *put the branks on someone* put someone in his place
breeks trousers
breenge dash around recklessly
brie-stane sandstone
brisket chest above ribs
brose porridge
brosey lumpen, clumsy
browdened on soft on
bude had to, must

ca' call, to carry out an action
ca' canny be careful
cadger tinker
canny clever
chaw humiliate
chirt grind
clachan small village
clarty dirty
clishmaclaver gossip
close tenement entrance
the College university
cowp overturn
cowte colt
crack gossip
creepie stool
creeshy greasy
cuddie donkey, a fool
cutty short pipe

dander stroll
darg toil
daudin falling on
daurna dare not
deil devil
dirl shudder
dominie teacher
doos pigeons
douce kind, gentle
dowp arse
dree endure
drucken drunken
dub puddle

e'en eyes; evening
Embro Edinburgh
ettle expect

fa' owre fall asleep
feck a lot
fliskie lively girl
flyte scold, abuse verbally
forbye also, besides
fornenst opposite, before
fosie dim-witted
fou drunk
fows who's (N.E. dialect)
foy celebration
fuff sputter

gae go
gang go
gar make, compel
gate way
gaun going
gawcey happy, prosperous
gerse grass
gey very, awful
gey pickle quite a lot
geyly considerably
gie give
gill-stoup bar in a pub
glaikit stupid

gleg sharp-witted
glower glare
golder shout
gowan daisy
gowk idiot; cuckoo
gowl yell
gowsterous wild, boisterous
groset gooseberry
gunkit disappointed, tricked
gurly bad-tempered

hadden doon oppressed
haet atom
hained gear clothes that are well looked after
hairst harvest
haver talk nonsense
headrig turning space at the top of a ploughed field
heavy-footed pregnant
herd shepherd
hirpled limped
holm field
host cough
hotch jump
howff pub
howk dig
hunkers haunches
hunks slob
hurdies hips
huts hoots (as in 'hoots, mon')

ilka every, each

jalouse consider, think
jaup splash with mud
jing-bang the whole lot
jo joy, darling
jocose merry
John Barleycorn whisky
jouk cheat, dodge
joukery-pawkery trickery

kane roughly 1800 kilos
keek quick look
ken know
ke-o shambles
kimmers women
kist chest, box

Lammas August 1st
lang-syne long time ago
lauch laugh
linn waterfall
linty linnet
lippen to depend on
lowe flame
lug ear

Martinmas November 11th
maun must
mavis songthrush
mim prim
mowdie-man molecatcher
muckle much, a lot
mutch woman's cap

nain own
nebby cheeky, nasty
novelles sentimental stories
the now at present

ocht anything
oom eh?
or before
orra-man odd-job man
owre over, too
owre-by over there

pack friendly
parratch porridge
pelter downpour
pickle a few
ploy entertaining plan
pow head
powney pony

pree imbibe
preen pin
prig plead
puddock stool toadstool

quean girl

rag-folk tinkers
redd up clear away
reek smoke
rone guttering
rowp auction
rype remove

sairly badly
saugh-wand willow branch
scunner disgust
sederunt meeting
shaw trimming
shilp thin, poor, ill-fed lass
sic thus
siller money
skelloch scream
skelp bash on, hit
skirl scream
slabber slob
slaik wipe down
smeddum guts
smeowt insignificant person
sneck-drawer sly sneak
snirt snorted laugh
snoove glide away
sonsy nice
spae foretell
speir ask
splash-brods mud-guards
splore let slip
spunk energy
spunkie a likely lad
stell stop
stot bullock
stots leaps
stour dust

stravaig wander
streek stretch
stunt stamp
sumph idiot
swankie show-off
swatch small piece
sweer, swure swear, swore

tack rent
tacketty hob-nailed
tattie-walin selecting potatoes
tawse strap
thae those
thir these
thole suffer
thowless spiritless
thrang pressure
thrapple throat
trauchle poor thing
tweesh between
tyuts toots (as in 'hoots-toots')

unco great, strangely
upsides wi' on the same level as

warstle wrestle
wat wet
waur worse
weird fate
whalp whelp
whaur where
wheen a few, some
wheeple whistle
whigmaleerie silly notion
winna would not
wintled tumbled
wud mad

yean whoa
yestreen yesterday
yett gate
yill ale
yon that

TEACHING AIDS

The Schools and Further Education Committee of the ASLS has produced a Lesson Pack of approximately 150 pages. It contains notes, units and worksheets for the whole range of the secondary school. Some of the topics covered are:

The House with the Green Shutters, *The Prime of Miss Jean Brodie*, the poetry of Sydney Goodsir Smith, junior fiction and a substantial unit on language. (The pack is colour-coded for insertion into the Jordanhill Scottish Language and Literature Project). £4.00

ASLS Commentary Cassettes

The following audio cassette commentaries have been produced and are now available:

Sunset Song by Douglas Young	£3.00
'The House with the Green Shutters' (A) Tone by Ian Campbell	£3.00
'The House with the Green Shutters' (B) Characterisation by Ian Campbell	£3.00
'The Silver Darlings' by Douglas Young	£3.00
R.L. Stevenson's 'Thrawn Janet' and 'Markheim' by Ian Campbell	£3.00
Hogg's 'Confessions of a Justified Sinner' by Douglas Gifford	£3.50
Fourteen Poems of Sorley Maclean by Iain Crichton Smith with readings by Sorley Maclean	£3.50
Three Poems of Burns by R.D.S. Jack ('Tam O'Shanter', 'John Anderson my Jo', and 'Holy Willie's Prayer')	£3.00
Seventeen Poems of Edwin Morgan by Roderick Watson with readings by Edwin Morgan	£3.50
Nineteen Poems of Norman MacCaig by Edwin Morgan with readings by Norman MacCaig	£3.50
Two Short Stories of Carl MacDougall by Elaine Petrie with readings by Carl MacDougall	£3.00

SCOTNOTES

Study guides to major Scottish writers and literary texts

Produced by the Schools and Further Education Committee of the Association for Scottish Literary Studies

Series Editors
Lorna Borrowman Smith
Ronald Renton

Editorial Board
Ronald Renton, St Aloysius' College, Glasgow
(Convener, Schools and Further Education Committee, ASLS)
William Aitken, Stevenson College, Edinburgh
Jim Alison, HMI (retired)
Gerard Carruthers, University of Strathclyde
Alistair Chynoweth, The High School of Dundee
Dr Morna Fleming, Beath High School, Cowdenbeath
Professor Douglas Gifford, University of Glasgow
John Hodgart, Garnock Academy, Kilbirnie
Alan MacGillivray, University of Strathclyde
Dr James McGonigal, University of Glasgow
Rev Jan Mathieson, University of Edinburgh
Lorna Ramsay, Fairlie
Dr Kenneth Simpson, University of Strathclyde
Lorna Borrowman Smith, Wallace High School, Stirling

THE ASSOCIATION FOR SCOTTISH LITERARY STUDIES aims to promote the study, teaching and writing of Scottish literature, and to further the study of the languages of Scotland.

To these ends, the ASLS publishes works of Scottish literature; literary criticism and in-depth reviews of Scottish books in *Scottish Studies Review*; short articles, features and news in *ScotLit*; and scholarly studies of language in *Scottish Language*. It also publishes *New Writing Scotland*, an annual anthology of new poetry, drama and short fiction, in Scots, English and Gaelic. ASLS has also prepared a range of teaching materials covering Scottish language and literature for use in schools.

All the above publications are available in return for an annual subscription. Schools can receive teaching materials by joining ASLS at a special reduced rate. Enquiries should be sent to:

ASLS, c/o Department of Scottish History, 9 University Gardens, University of Glasgow, Glasgow G12 8QH.

Telephone/fax +44 (0)141 330 5309
e-mail d.jones@asls.org.uk
www.asls.org.uk